'If death surrounded you, where would you go? What would you bathe in to heal your wounds? What weapons would you use to fight the darkness and light your way? Maybe you would visit the sea. Maybe you would rub salt into your cuts. Maybe you would write poetry. Sussi Louise Smith does all of the above, with heart-breaking honesty and laugh out loud imagery' *Eleanor Snare; Writer, Speaker and Superhuman.*

'Most of the time, poetry is a window into the poet's soul. But in *Seashaken light*, Sussi Louise Smith hands you a mirror and makes you travel into your own, because she is not just a poetess or a child of the sea. She is a witch, who packed sunsets, silence, the sound of waves, snow and immortality into a bottle, that she is handing over, for you to take a sip. You'll taste it, and you will ask for some more.' *Johana Gustawsson, Award-winning author of Block 46, Keeper and Blood Song.*

'Achingly tender and raw, Seashaken Light is truly a siren's song of the sea and love, but also of the fragility of life with illness and hope that still endures. It moved me, like the waves, shaking me while also bringing joy.' *Pernille Hughes, bestselling Author of Punch Drunk Love & Probably the Best Kiss in the World.*

'What do you get when you mix a sea lover with the cruel storms of cancer? Unbridled hope. With her poignant, authentic voice Sussi takes us on an unforgettable journey, reminding us that there is healing hope in the seashaken light over broken waters. She shows us that even if we are shaken, there is freedom and hope enough to go round. Lyrical waves of compassion, truly inspiring. ' *KM Herbert author of Book of Moons*

Sussi Louise Smith

Seashaken Light

- An ode to the shores we love

Foreword by Cape Cod Seascape Artist Tjasa Owen

Catherine Harper Publishing

Printed by PIXARTPrinting, Venice, Italy
Copyright © Sussi Louise Smith
All rights reserved
Catherine Harper Publishing

Text set in Times New Roman
Printed in Italy
First edition 2020
ISBN 978-0-9957512-1-7

For the sea, she always knows what to say
and for David, who always knows what to do

Foreword

Gosh, what the sea means to me….

It's my soulmate,

and anyone who feels the same, is dear to me and understands me clearly.

It is hard to formulate in words,

really,

the sea is more of an emotion to me

- I paint it and Sussi Louise writes it…

so beautifully real.

Full of sand and storms.

It is all there.

The Laughter, the rain,

the hurt

and the fresh start after the storm

I loved the journey, if you are a sea lover,

I am sure you will too.

Love xx

Tjasa Owen,
August 2020

Contents

Introduction

I knew from the first moment I opened my eyes that I was a child of the sea. Dry land never felt like home to me. Even as a baby, I remember crawling through the sand into the water, tasting the salt and sensing the grit, my mother relentlessly trying to stop me. Since keeping me away from wet stuff was proving impossible, teaching me how to swim seemed logical. It was no surprise to anyone that I spent most of my time under the surface. That is still where I am most comfortable. One of the biggest disappointments in my life is that I have not yet cracked how to breathe under water. There is a deeper sense of belonging for me there. Or on it. Or in it. Even by it will do.

During my childhood in provincial Denmark we spent all holidays and every weekend sailing. If the ice on the fjords in winter was not too thick, we would be out sailing then too. That is how my heart has come to work best, on the frequency of the salty seas. Fresh water somehow doesn't cut it. So, it is only natural, that when my family started disappearing into their next adventures, led by cancers and dementia, I turned to my oldest friend, the sea.

My oldest friend may be the sea, but my husband David is my first true love. He is the person that inspires and pushes me to always be the best I can possibly be. It is not right, and it is not fair, but he has health challenges too. Not the sort that kill you straight away, but those that can wear you down slowly. All I want is to be his light keeper, shelter him from it all. I try, but living next to someone who is ill, it is particularly important to take care of your own light too. Hope is such a filigree thing, but she is made of titanium. I promise. Mortality and immortality are ongoing themes in my stories, and they always end up by a lighthouse, under a stormy moon, blowing in promise and sparkle. Best way to combat challenges, I find? Laugh.

The words in here may be raw at times, but hopefully you can relate and hear the hope and humour too. If my plan works out, you can feel that shining through as you read.

Sussi Louise, the Landlocked, Yorkshire Dales, 2020

And So It Begins

And so it begins
with a sunset

Almost behind the end of the sea
but not quite

Rusty tangents seeking their escape to me
I am right here,
as ever.
Open heart.

Ready for the last cry of light

This is how it always begins
with a sunset,
a sea
and my open arms

Seashaken Light

– Song to the North Sea

Seashaken
Breaking
the boundaries of a world not yet known.

Underwater icicles piercing
An ocean of ice picks pushing at the gate
All the gates

East coast winters
North Sea having its fill
Eating the rocks
The sand
The land

Not me though
The sea and I have an understanding
It can seashake me
But not sea-break me.
Not break

And in return I will breathe
overwater icicles
Toes and sea intangibles
I am here
Seashaken
Not breaking
Just breathing
at the gates

Land and sand
in fluid lines
I follow the sound of the
seashaken light that shapes me
Seaborn I am
Seaborne I will be
Me
Daughter of the blue mind Sea

Light Keeper

When the stars have faded, and you are pulling away
drawing your night sky deeper
your back to me, our lungs out of breath
I will be your light keeper
shelter you from the watershed
I will show you where to step

Let us rewrite the mares from the night
creating golden memories of days so eager
Scattering your visions of gasping grace,
my heart will breathe for yours
Just let me be your light keeper
I will carry you in your dreams too
Let me leave the light on for you

I will move the moon so you can see
we may not have all the time we need
but we have the now and, how we hold this fitful sleep
My love don't be afraid, let me have your light to keep
look at all the love we've made
It will help me shine our light

When the stars have faded, and you cry in your sleep
hanging on to the night sky so tight, your back to the day
I will weave flowers through your fear, chase away the reaper
shelter you from sun flares my dear
Let me be your light keeper
I will always shine our light so bright

The days can be so scary, the future so close to spent
that's what I hear in your heart at night, that time is such a fluid fight
But don't trust your dreams my love, we have eternities in sight
Let me be your light seeker,
painting fairy dust and magic seas, diving us into the galaxies
Let me, forever be, your love, your light, your keeper

Daughters of the Sea

Minute cool kisses of foam
blown from the sea
Coveted and created
we were born
in a wave of green transparency
My sisters and me
Daughters of the sea

And as the sea Gods spoke
of trials and wars
we learned
our ways and were granted our lungs
and legs
My sisters and me
Daughters of the sea

To walk shores in earnest
feeling the field but
not to plant roots
Still breathe the currents and rhythms
of our home horizons
My sisters and me
Daughters of the sea

Storms blow whispers from forests
beyond the golden waves
ripping the cloth of branches
and dancing the red blanket
Ready for
My sisters and me
Daughters of the sea

So we can return whole
Leaf by leaf leaping
From earth to salt
Lest we forget we belong to the breach
and the ocean

My sisters and me
Daughters of the sea

Still, dales lure us with tales
of quiet green surf
Love divine, true
Chestnuts call us, the rivers tell sagas
Then our own story seeks
me and my sisters
the daughters of the sea

So when fall comes calling
the sea Gods call too
Souls crying, pining
Calling gently, so gently reminding
us of where we belong
My sisters and me
Daughters of the sea

Home is where the sea roars
Home is in the draw of tide
The breaking, the beating
connecting us all beat by beat-beat
Surf by surf-surf
My sisters and me
We are daughters of the sea

Liquid Light in the Green Moon Sky

Your kitchen will be filled with the faint aroma of roses
soaking you all in joy.
The house will sigh for brighter nights and
shooting stars up high
Lavenders will drift right in
airborne with delight
This home will kiss you sweet goodnights
under the green moon light

The grace, the grace, the endless love
that comes with salty stars
blink, blink clarity of sweaty pearls on lips

Faint memories of not yet here
the forgotten future trips
They are all there by your kitchen sink
the daily dreams
right at your fingertips

The house remembers everything
cold shivers and the sun
The liquid languid days of fun
of rain that was never gone

Your kitchen is filled with sweet goodbyes
and longing tangled hair
The faint aroma of roses there
that lingers everywhere
There is no such thing as final farewells
and no one to steal your light
You'll meet again in the liquid light
under the green moon sky

Symphony

I have been hearing things
Whispers behind the shadows
Before, all I saw was silence
Not the average thunderous kind
The deeper-waters-run-calm kind

Building up a choir of
salty symphonies sweeping
Before, what I heard was all green
Not the chilled sarcastic kind
The no-man-is-an-island kind

The house on the hill cut loose
Floating high on hopeful notes
Before, all I sensed was fear
Not the hot and bothered kind
The knife-in-the-gut-kill-cut kind

No sinking on my watch, no
No unfulfilled crescendo
Before the finale I will feel
the great release from afar
Joining this haywire seaborne orchestra

I have been hearing things
blue whispers behind the moon
before, all I saw was music
not the silent build-up kind
no, the all-is-changed-forever kind

Pink Sea Moon

Skylarks falling asleep in their flight.
overhead, out of light
A new moon cradles wild strawberry snakes
little berries for little cakes
on picnic tables and plastic plates
Seagulls diving to catch a bite
but not tonight

This night is the night of a young pink moon
vainly smiling in mirror seas
and seals that bark in tune
Sea moons are like that, alluring
and altogether curing me
of any kind of rational thinking
They push it, eat it and make space
for magical beings and ancient singing

Leaf by Leaf Leaping

Ocean breeze lingers
Life might never remember
as I do
but he still dazzles me
Cavernous pools of stars
Drawing me through the moulting crowns
My blinded sky sailing down
leaf by leaf leaping

Rolling red carpet in waves
of hazy autumnal anticipation
Constantly blurring the line between
the Sea and me
We walk together on water
swim together in leaves
Stars are leading
blink by blink blinking

The fjords sail forward
They narrow the gap
As I
they are dazed by the promise
of salty kisses and kelp cleared senses
No freshwater softness here just
my soul and me, the daughters of the sea

Leaf by leaf leaping
I surf to his call
I'm on the river praying for him
to take me home
The sea God and his watery ways
summoning my passion
My wave and me, we are daughters of the sea

The ocean breeze teases
me back to this life
and he still dazzles me
With emerald pools of leading stars
he is drags me through the dales
My sails are full,
as I leaf by leaf leap
to my love and me,
we are the souls of the sea

The Monster Below

What monsters lie beneath this glass-like sea
                  that is me?

What deep unravelling does here happen?
                  between me and the Kraken?

The fury so fierce the seas split in two
                  I know it scares you
                          It scares me too

It is not just the size of this scaly thing
                  it is the power of the skin

I grow with it so huge,
                the moon and the stars disappear
                        in the turmoil of my fear

And only when I reach the sun
                it is gone

I am a Daughter of the Sea

I am a daughter of the sea
I am more than that
I am you I am me
I am a daughter of the sea

You are a king of the sea
You are more than that
You are me you are you
You are a king of the sea

The waves are our language
They speak in all tongues
The tiny vibrations
The thunderous ones

We are all sea-folk
We are more than that
We are them we are us
We are all sea-folk

Under the surface and
under that still
underwater underworlds
under the sea we mill

I am a daughter of the sea
I float and fare
I dive and dare
I am a daughter of the sea

This Sea in Me

It may not look like much
        this dark water across from me
it may be frosty in its response
             but it does listen
             just wait and see

This water, this body
            across from me

We've had this conversation
           a million times
It calls for me
           it howls and cries
           but when I arrive
            the cool nod
like the old dog,
          when I've been gone
too long,
           refusing to say hello

It may not look like much
        this dark sea across from me
It may be limited in its response
          but it listens you see
          it knows me, really
this sea,
           this sea in me

Green Moon Sea

All clouds in flight
dislodging and dodging
To make silvery way
for the green moon to stay

All stars are still
Composing and doting
Twinkling sea mirror true
reflect the moon and queue
                   (for you)

All waves they blow
breathing and receding
Waiting in quiet line
for the glory of emerald moonshine

All winds are glowing
unbreathing not sleeping
Counting out the sounds of grace
Stars alight, the moon at full blaze

All touch is shining
beating and reaching
High, yet deeply below
All the horizons in overflow

Our souls are sparkling
listening and whispering
ready to forever be
                   (unapologetically)
afloat in the green moon sea

The Song of Kraken

This is me
The daughter of the sea
Bathing amongst the trees
Reaching for the open crease
My legs buried deep below
That earthy crust of over-tow
It's not wrong but it's not right
This aquamarine moulting serpentine

This is me
This is I,
this Kraken underneath
swimming through the seas of time
Setting roots where fins once were
My gills all sandy, I'm growing fur
The precious scales are falling foul
of the forest people's respectful bows

This is me
I am the sea
Waving my way in-land
Riding the sea fog from coast to coast
Searching for that perfect repose
There is no distance
There is no time
Just this perfectly moulted serpentine

Sea of Stormy Stars

In the unseen sea of calm
above the stormy moon
She stretches her lanky tail and sings
with shooting stars and her zealous hope

In the *mahseh* by the sea
below the falling stars
he extends his true soul and responds
in azure sea curls and golden faith

The Gods are watching
taking in the splendour,
they gift the lovers an orchestra
a sea of stormy stars
so they can sing each other lullabies
to their souls' symphony

Rim Breath

There's a hole
where you were.
I stare into it for eternities
The air and music tell me where the edge is
There is only one

It's the space around the hole
that gets me
And the way it breathes
as if you were still here
Telling me stories
Tucking me in.

The flora and fauna changes as I walk the edge of you
You always loved the African violet roses
but didn't care for the thorns
'Who does', I used to say
'The birds', you would answer, *'they can hide from the cats'*

I don't even know if that's true, Mum
if you're not here to tell me.
Still, I told my own children the same story
and they believe me
Like I believed you
Until you made this hole
And made me make my own truths

It's ok, I should have done that decades ago
Really

As I walk the edge
at times
the only thing holding me up
and stopping me from dropping in, is
the wind blowing upwards.
Sometimes hot, making the flowers and trees bloom out of season
Sometimes cold. Covering me in mesmerising snowflakes
that don't even melt when I hold them in my open palm

Or on my fingertips.
You know I am in love with snow
I know, you still know that

Sometimes,
it's a sand-duned landscape
of warm summers
spent by the white and golden beaches of small islands
Naked I was
Sand in my teeth and every crevice
And in your bed
because there was no shower on the boat
At I wouldn't sleep without your breath on my neck

I still can't quite sleep without that
That is why I often rest by the hole you left for me
Feeling your love softly caressing my hair

Like when I was four
Before school
Before dad's affair
Before you didn't smile for years, but then you did again
You didn't stay in the hole.
Thank you.

But you did widen it a few times.
I watched you standing on the edge
Reminiscent of a siren in that perfect storm
Drawn to the sea
Torn between the urge to destruct and the
urge to love…
deciding to help the fishermen instead
And me
You stayed with me
With us…
Kissing us goodnight again
Brushing my long hair carefully
Not always patiently, but lovingly
Like mums do

As I was giving birth to my firstborn
You were there, soft-spoken

Calming me. Impossible me
For days I stood by my own hole
Not knowing what to do
Feeling like a failure.
I saw you
From up above
I saw us all
Me in sheer panic, you, stroking my hair
The doctors and midwives
I could see that you were talking to me,
but I couldn't hear a word
I was so close to the edge
and it took all I had not to let myself fall in
But you had me, held me here
I am sorry I couldn't save you back, mum.

The first time the cancer came
You were so brave
Bright eyed fighter spirit
Late afternoons playing cards
just you and I in the ward

The second time,
I saw you lose something
We looked everywhere,
or maybe you were lost?
You wouldn't let anyone in
It took years before you let me in again.
Years before I saw you step away from the rim again

I know now that you were
working, with all you had
That you were walking
patrolling your rim
to make your space safer
smaller
So you wouldn't fall in.
Surviving the best way you could.
I admire that

The third time cancer came
We both said hello

32

And we knew she had come to stay
So, we made her up a bed
But not in the living room
Down the hall,
a nice bed so she didn't get too angry
But not so nice she wanted to spend all the time decorating the room

She did so anyway,
Painted polka dots on your pretty lungs
And giraffe patterns in your liver
She made fireflies in your lymph nodes
And leopard prints on your skin
And in the end, she painted large images of night skies in your brain
And then
she had to leave
Your body was dead
And you left me too
Your time walking the rim of your breath was up and you let yourself fall
Your work here was done
Thank you
For this beautiful hole
The glorious landscapes you have spent so long making for me along the edge
The wind that keeps me here
That teaches me how to build my own rim breath
Shaping it through dance and watery breaths
I create castles and cinnamon buns on laden branches,
paintbrush fences and azure coloured air
For my children when they might visit there
I plant wishing wells and build sweet honeysuckles
Forming dreams and hammock retreats
among friendly fireflies and gentle bees
The dark mountains look beautiful from here
But don't go there

When it is my time, I hope my children will see
All the stories that make up the air that is me
Just like I do
when I dangle my feet over the edge of your space, Mum
Your breath tickles my baby toes
This feeling never goes away.
The mother, the child
Rim breaths and thousand memories

Beneath the Wake

What stories lie below these curling breakers and shell-like surfs?
Where does this watery road lead us?
Salty spray sparkled bonfire story times,
magic cockle whispers luring us closer to the sea
In the morning, the pit still warming sand and cold birds

Our home is now empty
The fish bones by the side
We loved it here
We dived right in

But now we are pulled again
Chasing wild swims and wild feathers
Further ashore still further offshore
Swimming deeper and deeper yet
Drawn to that true embrace, our monsters
and marvels tell our stories beneath the wake

Our home is now here
The fish swim by our side
We belong for sure
We dive right in

Underwater tales fresh from the curling breakers
This is where the watery road ends
No bonfire magic cockle whispers here
No, in this place their store ring loud and clear
The magic is now above us, still warming sand and sea birds

Footprints

The cool cliffs of Caroline
Leave not a trace of me
Wet footprints linger just a bit
Then fade so gingerly

Our paddle prints from the swims we took
The chalk hearts that we drew
Are eaten by the hungry sun
And washed away by dawn

We are the Waves

Into the ending summer's blossoms
and out of the dog-roses' prickly shade
these itchy trails of playing with berries we were told not to touch
Like Adam and Eve, we fill our bellies with forbidden fruits
This is no Eden though,
this is no walk in the park
The blossoms cover us like snow
all mixed with sticky kelp and
sea-fret salty bitterness

We are the waves and
when you move, I move too
Not always in your direction
Not ever out of fear

I move in love
In love with the way your body flows
The way it claims its space
The respect you show the beautiful lawns
and cracks in the pavement alike.

A space around you glows
covered in salty crystals and slightly curled evening petals.
And behind that space is midnight star sparkled calm
That perfect pinhead balanced place of sadness and pure love
I know this place well
And when you're tiptoe dancing on the break of the wave,
I dance too, surfing through

We are the waves,
the world of ways that we are linked
but still not one we move
Across seas and the oceans
hidden below them too
Running with the deepest currents
And resting in the shallows
Breathing with you
And when you dive, I dive in tune
Empowered by love and enveloped by truth

The Colour of Hope

All at once the colours go from autumn warm to iceberg cool
With every breath the hues are stolen
Tucked away for safekeeping
All at once the world slows down
reverts its motion redirects the notion that anything is the same
and slowly the beginnings of a centripetal maelstrom,
pregnant with glorious density,
starts its swirly ways

This is how we survive the pain
This is how we survive all the living we are committed to

Focus
Leave the colours for a while
Dig under the pretence and awkward smiles
The quiet that can only be found
under the icebergs of what we thought were endless times

The pain that tears us apart
The sin, the punishment, the Eden curse
Pulling away all sense of sense
and clarifies the mind like a vintage wine
The tunnel, the screams are all in our heads.
And the maelstrom is picking up the pace

To our surprise we see right there
at the bottom of the earth sea floor
Hope

She's dressed so exquisitely
Her dress
her hair
floating like in the sea
Soft turquoise in her eyes and breath
She's picks us up and gingerly
carries us away from a sweet drowning death

The earth stands still yet again

Reverts, revolves and changes its shade of grace
Now outwards spinning
We're clinging on to the scalp of the world we know
Pulling out her hair
And she responds with explosions of colours
the icebergs are literally
and figuratively melting
and we regain the blushing in our cheeks

This is how we live
This is the colour of Hope
This is how we survive
This is how we survive.

The Shape of Hope

Every cell screams to be set free
Like a dying person begging for loved ones to let her go
So she can float away
find her rhythm in the waves within the calmer Elysium
Until she is chosen once more to do her job
here on earth
or maybe somewhere else
I could be the Nordic Amazonian fighting her way
The sailor of moonlit seas and an untired purveyor of hope
I could swim with the meanest of Krakens

But can I do this?
I'm not sure I can do this.
I don't know. Anything much anymore

I used to think I knew things
I used to think there was meaning in most things
Maybe there is
Maybe it is just me
I might have lost my ability to believe or
maybe the gods have lost their patience with me,
or worse
perhaps there altogether never existed such magical things as meaning or gods?
I don't know. Except that I don't know.
Socrates is not wasted on me; I buy in completely.

My eyes seek the shapes of the things I know are there
The guileful contours of fleeting recognition
Murmurs moving the light just out of reach
Persistent whispers of hope pleading for release
I see her behind the thin veil

She is a sinewy creature, Hope
looks frail and filigree,
But do not be fooled
her intricate structure is lovingly created from the finest titanium
She may be little, but she holds on with fierce delicacy,
and within the humming of our heartbeats

she paints bursts of summer blue skies
blinding sunshine on moon fallen snow
She sings lullabies with the healing sounds of diamond glitters
on calm ocean currents
and the first laughs of breastfed babies
Reminding us softly of all that is light and love
as she breathes her blessings next to our daytime nightmares
She keeps us here until it's time to go.
Because
When Hope is gone
What else is there to do but follow?

I can't do this, but I also can't not do it.
I am risen, but not yet awake
The veil, too thin for comfort
One foot in the world of the living the other amongst the stars

The outline of my garden reappears through the morning haze
shadows moving so slowly they show the waves of love in the depth of his eyes
If he wasn't there, would I be here?
I honestly don't know
I don't know
And the shame is killing me
Who am I to think like this?
How ungrateful to let myself be led by desperation?
The desperation blinked into existence by physical pain and darker demons yet
Where is Hope when I need her the most?
She is the one thing I want to take with me everywhere
If my house were on fire, I would only save her.
The joy of life she brings on the darkest of nights
Entering any burning house to get her out, makes all the sense in the world
If we are to burn, let us burn with Hope in our eyes

I know how panics can lie
With their long thin fingers
they sing persuasive myths
from the far coasts of nightmares.
Soon, soon I am out of their grasp
I know this
Because I have been here so many times before
But right now
I am weakened, my body reels from the anguish and screams for help

All I need is hope
Hope, please come quick, I need your magic now.
Tell me about the cool swims in the Atlantic and the sultry nights of love making
Remind me how a hot summer feels
and how dancing on the beach under the quiet moon caught our souls unawares
Bound us together for all lives before and after this
Paint my wretched body in colours of the sea and let me feel your touch once
more.

Let me say that I can do this
With the trust that I can

I can do this
I can do this

Liquid Light

A tale of the English summer

There's a quality of magic
in this darkness of summer sun
The liquid light we bathe ourselves in
caresses us through our oilskins
The battle between our light and the fog, fighting clouds

I am not here for the eternal sun or the brightness of your moon
The magic is what draws me into this summer cool
Balmy nights of silvery promises
of an end to these days drowning us in perpetual liquid sunshine

Fairies, dragons and insomnia
The endless wakeful dreams of far off universes
Where summer means sun
Toes in hot sand and drinks by the riverbanks
Not this liquid light we bottle for bitter gins,
to soothe our gloom come winter

I don't believe in umbrellas
or in death
I don't even think I believe in God anymore
But I do believe in sunlight, liquid or otherwise
I know it's there and give me a moment
eyelids gently shut
and I can almost feel it on my skin

Bottled Sunsets

Bottled sunsets and summers' gold
on my buttered toast in the winter
Memories of naked swims and sandy ears
and rosehip rashes on still pale skin

Mood-lifter magic in a jar
Strawberry jam on warm pancakes
Taste buds reaching out for endless summer light
And rosehip syrup on top

I am Dust

I feel the stale air seeping through my wary mind
The dust diamonds locked in mid-air like
snowflakes whispering secrets of no-good housewives

I am frozen
I can freeze time
It is an 'almost' superpower
this sharp clear ice sight ultra-vision

I am still in my pyjamas.
The house is still asleep
I probably should be too
But I am spending my time studying the dust suspended in air
caught in the battle between me and the rising sun

I lock them in time with my start-starry eyes
And while I do,
my ears wander off, filled with hunger for adventure.
The nose is not far behind,
like an annoying little sibling always wanting to tag along with the big ones.
I know where they are going,
I don't need to strain my mind
It is where I would go too,
if I weren't in the middle of the weightless battle of the specks

The sea, the sea
I hear the waves before they are even there, the ears, and
only a short second behind I get overwhelmed by the fearless aroma caught by Nose.
Salty sea and stale shallow waves rocking in the languid summer sunrise
The seaweed already steaming
Rotten grass of the ocean floor
reminding us all who is king below and above
Water in all its shapes will rule the world to the end
The wind picks them all up and scolds them for leaving their master.
That is me, he thinks
He has no idea.

44

For a second there I feel them all blush
Though they soon forget and go exploring
riding on the back of the fresh breeze that found them.
Shrieking in happiness as they hit an air hole and drop,
free fall, towards the ground

I sense all this.
As I am deadlocked in the battle of me, the light and the dust mites
Sat on the sofa in my old morning gown
With the house still asleep
my skin is prickling with the touch of every breath
the soft feel of the flannel pyjamas
The dust diamonds are unimpressed; they just hang there in the ray of light
Tied up by my superpower and the sun
I can almost taste the smell of their existence
Mixed up with the scent of burnt toast and overripe bananas
This bad housewife situation is taking no prisoners
Everyone is in the pot for a reshuffle
Time tastes different when you are too tired to blink

The ears are back squealing with happiness
telling tall tales of sea creatures knowing their names
They are twins but their experiences are so different
Right, saw Poseidon and swam in his foamy breath
Left, dived under sapphire ceilings, was fed fat oysters by graceful mermaid hands
Nose, is, as always, all over the place. It's all too much, she needs a nap

I give up
And release the dust to flow and flutter
Dance their merry ways to my windowsills and
tops of cupboards for my cloth to find
Sometime
Not today, today I am invincible
Sat in my old sofa
at dawn
whilst the world is still asleep

The Unseen

In this landscape
       of epically
           important
               decisions
    Visibility is a
          thousand
      meters
    Every detail is
      as clear
        as
  Yet
    I am
    in despair.
The road
    I thought
      was mine
        is nowhere to be seen

For ages the fog has hidden
          the contours
             only shown the peaks
               but I knew it was all there
Now I can see
    everything
      and
        I
          am
            lost
Confused
  Blinded by windy
      shades
        and shapes
          of what colours
            I thought
              I knew were there
We are all here
    unseen?

All for Me

Poem for Daisy (aged 3)

All the grass is golden
All the sea is green
All the sky is purple
And all this is for me

The roses sing in thorny tune
The skylarks they compete
The porpoise whistles longingly
And all this is for me

In the shadow berries reach
In the sun the leaves
In the wind the dragonflies
And all this is for me

It has got to be
this beauty spree
I've prayed for it so long
So, this I'm sure,
has got to be
at least a bit for me

I Don't Understand the Butterflies

Poem for Zia (aged 8)

I don't understand the butterflies
The way they fly is weird
Their wings are so big and so paper thin
I know this
Cos I kissed one and then it couldn't fly
I cried I cried and mummy told me
it would have to die
I don't understand butterflies
They can´t be petted or caressed
Even a kiss can mean their death
And still they fly and flim flutter fly
as if they don't even know to try
to escape, me

Dad says butterflies are breakfast animals
And that's why they are called butter f l i e s
onto your toast
and in scrambled eggs
Butter on all the things we eat.

Mum says butterflies are not animals at all
they are magical little creatures
like fairies, and angels and kind little things.
Their lives are so short they can taste with their feet
That should have made me smile but
that made me so sad
Not at all glad
Cos I killed one when I tried to be good
So, I don't understand butterflies

Don't Listen to Sad Me

It's not true.
Don't listen to me
I've made all the wrong turns
Seen so many wrong roads
My mind tells me stories of
things I can't do
And places I should have gone
But it's not true
So, don't listen to that me
The wrong turns and dark roads were all there to guide
They haven't made me crazy
not sure they made me stronger
But I know they made me me
And I am okay
I did the best I could
with the hand that I was given

I was a protective mother and a lover of friends and life
No money to pay for any extras
Or even just meat
But I learned to cook a carrot in a hundred ways
Flavoured with seaweed and nettles,
wild garlic and bramble berries
Spices from nature, the larder of Gaia

So, It's not true
Don't listen to sad me
She's made of guilt and of fight
She was the survivor between us
She didn't do gratitude meditations
or pray to a God that was clearly already too busy.
No, she fought,
nails sharp and teeth bared
She made spaghetti with tins of tomato
and rye bread open sandwiches topped with end-cuts of whatever protein.

She read the children sellotaped books from her own childhood

Still so young, she remembered all the little games and songs
And she cried
Cried tears of frustration
then kicked and kicked and demanded more
of herself and of me
Time and again we worked through the night
Studied, sleep deprived and hungry
She made sure I am here.
Fed, educated, warm
Happy in my own company
Loved

But she doesn't need to fight for survival anymore
It's not true
So, don't listen to her
I am on the right path
I always was on a different path than the generations before me
A different path than my siblings, at least

Wrong turns that somehow
were adventures and potent reminders of how grand life could be
How poles apart a life can be
Even when it is limited, restricted, small.
It is still life

Was I a good mother? I honestly don't know
Did I keep my young safe? Yes
Did I love them? More than life itself
Did I make mistakes? Certainly, tons
Could I have done differently? Possibly... almost certainly
if I had known more, understood more
But I did the best I could, she did.
She saved us and now ...

I am not hungry, I sleep at night, the children are no longer children.
I am no longer the warrior and purveyor of shelter.
I am me, too. All is good
So, don't listen to her
Maybe dare the prickliness of her hedgehog mind and give her a hug.
She did so well
My me before me

Where Do You Go When You Sleep?

Sometimes I look at you while you are sleeping
and I can hear the half-moon moans in your chest
Is that your star-lit soul, fighting your way home?
Where is home to you?

I watch you while you are dreaming
and I watch the silent flutter of your eyes
Is that your wings taking you away from me?
Where is it that you go?

Sometimes I see your tears while you sleep
and I collect them in an old jam jar
Are they your fireflies from beyond?
leading you the way
Which way are you going?

Where is it you go to when you are asleep?
And why won't you take me with you?
Where is it you live when you are dreaming?
And why can't I come with you?
Who is it that makes you cry when you're there?
And why can't I catch your tears?

Let me in, my fierce sky will keep you safe
I have a jar of fireflies
and a heart of golden dreams
So wherever you go when you need sleep
let me in it's all better than it seems

Landscapes

I hate this semi-existence of navigating through landscapes of pain
Since I am neither geographer, nor daredevil explorer
I prefer my GPS set on smooth waters and seaside adventures
Not saying a good storm can't catch my attention
or that the breaking of waves
against rugged East Coasts isn't scarily exhilarating, sometimes
but this day to day landscape of pain is not even a semi-existence, is it?

It a non–something
Like me
On those days

I do love the semi-existence
of navigating through landscapes of hope, though
Hope is such an innocent feeling
Makes me believe I still have a touch of naïveté about me
It's a fiction perhaps
But it's ok

'Everything is going to be just fine' I whisper
I know I am lying, he knows it too
But we both hope I am right
And if I am wrong,
we can't hear it for the roar of the ocean
making its way inland to save us
Because that's what it's doing, surely?

Hugging the landscape of life in all its many glories
and thorny crowns.
The pain, the hopes, the dreams, the skylark elegant patterns of
sandy beaches not walked on since the last storm

Our footprints barely lingering as the sea soothes our past

Love is not a Feeling

Not a hot winter's afternoon or
A chilly summer's eve
Love is not a feeling, not a feeling, not at all

Love is a truth
It is two truths
It is endless truth
Profound and prolific knowing
Core appreciation, genuine admiration
The rawest kind of respect

Love is not a feeling, not a feeling not for me
It is everything
it is truth
It is us
It is me
It is not
Or maybe it is

Love is not a feeling
not the fear that makes me small
not the lust that tears me up
Love is not a feeling, not at feeling, not at all

What it is, is all-consuming
Love doesn't take a lot
It takes it all
And then some more for a rainy day

No, love is not a feeling
Not just a feeling
Not at all

The Things We Love

(Inspired by my community of followers on Instagram)

Butterflies and forest bathing at dawn
Dandelions in the sky
Oceans, puddles, the sea and all things river
Grass covered in morning dew moving like wandering waves too
Friends in all places
Both high and here

Puppies and cooking, but not cooking puppies
Rainbows in chakra style
across waterfalls and tender hearts
all the children asleep but still holding hands
and my grandchild's arms around my tired neck

Rainy skies and skies stuck in trees
Masks on masks unmasking
Nature at its grandest and
above all, the sea, the sea, the sea
cliffs and rocks in open spaces
The sun all set to set again

The joy of books and books with books on top
And a perfectly symmetrical sandwich
next to a tall gin and tonic mid afternoon
Waking early and walking into the blue across the moors
and in the middle of the open roads
music every step Sibelius seducing us in Finlandia,
nodes gently caressing my soul, then waking me with
Vaughn Williams and a spot of Ella Fitzgerald

Laughter of true belonging mixed with the calm scent of morning coffee
The sweet smell of a baby's head and
Sunshine on already warn asphalt
Shaping like the petroglyphs on Ilkley Moor
Long-lasting love, new love, the love, all the love
And lots of mugs of tea
From a thermos, poured on the forest floor
On the edge of the heather

The comfort of friends, the family kind
Sharing the bliss of that open road
Taking us to the sea, the sea, the sea
The soothing sound of a lover's voice
And the kids out barefoot to get in trouble
They feel the freedom too
Wonder women on peace patrol
Long baths when I am home alone
While Optimus Prime guards the universe
We are all safe now

Silky knitting in my sofa corner
Big woolly jumpers comforting smoke in the air
Drunk honeybees too tired to swarm
Cuddles on the sofa
Some say puppies are happiness, some say cats
but it is books, we all know it
And the sea, the sea, the sea

A thousand shelves, with thousands of books
Painting all the colours of love, the love, all of the love
Paintbrushes, paints, pens and markers
Blank canvases and those with stories to re-tell
Memories and soft dreams
Freshly ironed sheets on my freshly made bed, and me in it
B That sense of autumn. The 'just right' kind of decay,
The type that smells of possibilities and hope
Or chocolate

And some even long for the perfectly shaped cacti
Me, I long for you, you by the ocean at sunrise
Cornish rolling hills, rolling straight into the waves
The dunes the beaches the riverbeds
Blackberries in my babies' hands and on their happy faces
more in their bellies than in their basket
That perfect garden bench, in that perfect spot
Looking at the village fair on a sunny day
The circus full of magic
Like new moons and bluebells in early spring
And did I say, the sea, the sea, always the sea

It Seems

It is not what it seems
Anything
Practically everything
The white on the ground
is not frost
The blue on the horizon
is not sky

This mile you see is not
for this moment
And the steady hum
of the earth's turning
is
not just for you

It is not
Whatever we think it is
It is changing
All is changing
No
Disappearing
Into spaces we cannot hold
not at all

The waters have spoken
This is their time
The oceans taking their sweet revenge
Nothing will be what it was again
What it seemed

Now I Can't Make It Snow

When it started, I could move the stars, the sun
Make it run, go or come
And now I don't even know how to make it snow
Cool your fears, make us grow
It is not a regular occurrence
this irregular disturbance

It's just that I need to be invincible,
hold you tight and be unsurpassable, spiritual
be your saviour or maybe just your light
But oh your gaze is anthracite
It is not a regular occurrence
this irregular disturbance
And I can't even make it snow
Cool your fears in frosty tableaus

It is just that you are the one
And I need you to know
 just before you are gone
That I dream of being your superhero
Play you an eternal diamond sparkling libero
But I no longer can make it snow
cover you in that silvery glow
 to make you my eternal king
and reach so far
we reach within

The frost, so frosty
preserves you
But
now
I can't make it snow

Decisive Pain

It knows what it wants
It carries me held high into the blinding sunlight
My body frail and folding every fibre around itself
It knows not what to do, but
the pain
This decisive pain
It knows where it is going
Reminding the specks of me of the whole I can be
The time that is now, is nothing like the now with the pain
A grandiose maelstrom, a cantankerous sea
Carrying me held high into the blinding sunlight
Above the cloud cover
and even over that
Far beyond this collection of matter,
beyond anything I have ever known
yet with the comfort of nothing new
it is safe here
in the arms of this decisive pain
at least I know that
if I die
I have felt everything and the nothingness
all at once
The trick is to let go
To go with the current, not fight against it
It's illogical
swimming towards sure pain and fear of dying
makes no sense
still
it is the only thing that makes sense
Letting it carry me safely, held high, into the blinding sunlight
It knows what it wants
Not like me
Who only knows what I don't want
But
With the sunlight warming my body the waves rocking me to sleep
The puzzle that is me starts to solve itself
The jigsaw pieces seek each other out
And

Slowly, I become me again.
The earth-side me,
One last big squeeze and I am sat
by my table, not quite knowing how I got here
writing words on salty pages
the grace of pain
it knows what it wants and maps out my escape routes
I do love that it knows

Cape Cod Seascape Painting by Tjasa Owen

Your colours made me cry
They broke my heart in that special way
The best way
No scarring
All healing

I heard the rumbling from the sea
The symphony of little clicks
That every grain of sand makes when it shifts
I felt the shift
Shift something in me

The colour of your rooftop hues
Is a deep hum
The kind you hear sitting back against an ancient tree
The kind of blue that if you look at it too long
You drift away, to far, far off places
Other worlds of otherworlds
You may not want to fly back

Hold on to the golden reeds
Hold on to the clear sound of the hidden reds
Roots in a deep A tone here
Reaching up as well as down
Reaching in
Into my broken heart to heal me

Your colours broke my heart today
In that special way
The best way
Thank you

Tunnel Vision

You ever get that feeling
that your body remembers sides of thoughts you don't
that it refuses to collaborate and interact in a respectful manner?

Do you ever get the shortness of breath
that somehow reminds you of how you'd
imagine
it would be like to drown?

Do you ever get the sense of no-sense
Non-sense?

The heart racing to a beat of a far-off memory
trying to catch up
catch in on
not just the right thing
but the doing it right
but you can't really hear the instructions for the
sound of the roaring sea in your eyes

Like developing tunnel vision
Only the tunnel is pointing in the wrong direction and
you are missing the point

How does one cope with that?

I Love This Song

Let me sing you a song
A cockle cooing serenade
A retrograde inspection
The long hair of the dunes we walk, the talks we talk, the walks we walk
All on her head, the land-laying seabed
Let's braid her locks, the skylark flocks can help us
clock
the adder's teeth in time
The slinky, snaky path it takes
are ours to take, if we dare.
I dare.
We dare

Let me sing you a song
A school of sea-turtle fairy tales
All the scales of mermaids' tails,
braided into Miss Dunes long tresses.

Our hands touch during the walks we walk,
the talks we talk as we snake our ways like little kids
then a short eclipse,
it splits
and we're here.
Sea froth calling through every grain
our sandy names
but we are no longer the same
yet forever here
all the cockle cooing serenades
of our nights long gone
and those still to come

Oh, I love this song
I love this song

Gratitude List

Light nights
Dark mornings
Sun on my face
Hope
Chocolate
Beauty
Kisses
Sea fret
Love
Affirmation
Sometimes bacon
Always kindness
Appreciation
Care
Attention
Belonging
Rain on hot asphalt
Sun on salty waves
Hugs
More kisses
His voice
Smoked salty almonds
The smell of newly mowed lawn
And carrots straight from the ground
Let's move bacon down here
Carrots before bacon
Actually, substitute bacon with dedication
And navy blue
Midnight blue
And crisp white
Affection and
Deep orange
Sky blue
Sea blue
Deep blue
Blue Mind
All the blues
Deep humour
Dance

Me dancing
My heart moving like nobody is watching
That perfect song
Spinning around
And the perfect Mozart piece
A good book
A clever book
The smell of books
The smell of mum
The smell of my children
The smell of the sea
The sound of the sea
Sound of the waves
The wind through the dunes
Move the sea up the list
To number one
No, number two
Make love number one
Then the sea
And hope
And carrots
Laughter
The sun through the windows in the morning
Coffee and a book
Birdsong
Quiet
Salty liquorice
Ok swap bacon for salty liquorice
Petroleum
Being alone
The light on the beach on a far-off island
The smell of salty seas,
I moved that up already, right?
Positivity
White walls
White houses with sea views
All houses with sea views
Sea views
White dogs
Black dogs
Magic
Synchronicity

Love – again
Stars
Move stars to number three
Ok four
The moon
Shooting stars
Vanilla
Being seen
really seen
Films
David, moved David up next to love
Calm
Laughter with dear friends
Kisses – again
Sea folk
Otters
Otters =6
Porpoises
Smiles
Gold
Money in my account,
enough for all the food I need
Going to the cinema
Cooking for hours
Sailing ships
Art materials
Especially the best brushes
Dreams
Babies –
Put babies at number 9
Sex
How many number ones can I have?
The taste of Danish cucumbers
And strawberries
The feeling of a kind person brushing my hair
Night-time
Deep night time
Wood fires
No phones
Sunflowers as they are reaching for the sun
And my electric blanket,
I need a special category for that little sucker

Happiness in my warm bed
Playing cards past midnight with my friends from school
Writing with the urgency of needing oxygen
Move writing up to number seven
Friends
Kisses again
Art, art with light, and water
Tjasa Owen's art
Mary Oliver's poems
Silence
Skylarks
Old trees
Waves
A great bookshop
The writer Ib Michael,
so otherworldly but somehow
he still writes straight into my heart
Just for me
Like Liz Gilbert in Big Magic
Move the Big Magic book waaay up the list
There would be printed seashaken without
Big magic
Or Daring Greatly
Or my garden
More hugs, more dancing, more music
but most of all more love
More sea and more hope
And let's just add fairy lights
Because,
there are never enough fairy lights
Or cuddles
Also freshly ironed sheets with us in between
And even more love
Kisses on my neck when I didn't realise, he was standing behind me
A hand looking for mine as we walk on a dusty road
going nowhere special
Meditations at dawn sat on warm sand
knowing the day is going to be glorious
Before I am even up, feeling awake
I am so grateful
And bacon is back on the list
I think

Acknowledgements

I would like to thank the universe for always having my back. For making sure I am never hungry. Not physically, not spiritually. To my mum, she would have been so happy for me. She still is I'm sure. To my true love David, who drives me mad in his resolute trust in my special kind of magic. Thank you for always holding my heart so gently. I could not have asked for a more wonderful 2020 lockdown buddy. You are my light.

A special thanks to The Grove Bookshop in Ilkley, West Yorkshire. The best bookshop and people I know. You have made a huge difference to the English immersion experience, making me feel at home in my new country. Emma Hughes, your interpretations of my poems into music have blown my heart right open. I am so grateful to dance with you. Kayla Herbert, my favourite Canadian poet and Wednesday muse. I am honoured to know you.

Also thank you to my 'afar' friends. *Jyne Greenley* (CA), you teach me to love the darkness of the woods and still feel the depth of the sea. *Tjasa Owen*, (USA), your art hit me straight in the heart from the first painting I saw. You made me realise that my synaesthesia was not just an advantage but a miracle. Your paintings sound like my heart feels when it smells the sea. *Christine Onward* (AU), *Mary Collette* (USA) and *Suzy Wildwriter* (UK), your art and hearts inspire me every day.

I am the luckiest person. Blessed to have the most beautiful people in my life, people who I know think I am a bit quirky, but who are liberal with their humour, support, wit and genius. Their grace makes me feel that I have a voice and a place here. On this planet most importantly my children, biological and bonus ones. You keep me on my toes with laughter and worry. No one could bring me more joy. My dear friends in Denmark, you know who you are because we speak all the time and even when we do not, we do in our hearts. I miss you, but I do not feel apart from you. The Yorkshire Dales network I am so grateful for and who have welcomed me to this wet county with open umbrellas and cups of tea (and Gin). Ali (s), Angela, Amy, Anthea, Carol, Emling, Greg, Jane, Jean, Jo, Joseph, Jules, Liz, Lorac, Lucy, Marie, Michael, Nikki, Otter, Ruth, Ray, Rux, Sarah, Steve, Tim, Ulrike, Uzma and

Vibeke. My two book clubs, the Writers on the Wharfe and the Brave New Words Writing group (without whom insanity definitely would have set in by early May, 2020).

The glorious writers *Carmen Marcus* (UK) & *Johana Gustawsson* (F, UK, S, E) need an extra cheer. When I first moved inland, I thought I would not survive. I was home, but homesick for somewhere that no longer was. Carmen taught me that the sea is in me and my skin is where all my stories lie. We are sea sisters indeed. Johana is the beacon that shows me that everywhere is home even if nowhere is. She taught me that allowing even the scariest and emotionally challenging storylines to have their space and light is the only way to embrace one's darkness. You are the queen of Noir ma Cherie, merci.

Lastly, I simply have to extend an extra big thank you to Mari, childhood friend and chronicler of my most distant memories. She told me to write poetry again. I have. I did. Thank you, my love.

There are many more to thank, and I am sorry if your name is not here. It is in my heart, I promise.

Sussi Louise Smith 2020